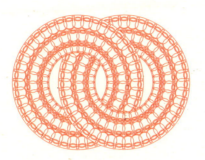

PELTED

BY

FLOWERS

PELTED

BY

FLOWERS

KALI

LIGHTFOOT

CAVANKERRY
PRESS

CavanKerry Press Ltd.
Fort Lee, New Jersey
www.cavankerrypress.org

Publisher's Cataloging-In-Publication Data
(Prepared by The Donohue Group, Inc.)
Names: Lightfoot, Kali, author.
Title: Pelted by flowers / Kali Lightfoot.
Description: First edition. | Fort Lee, New Jersey : CavanKerry Press, 2021.
Identifiers: ISBN 9781933880860
Subjects: LCSH: Lesbianism—Poetry. | Recovering alcoholics—Poetry. | Park rangers—Poetry. | Families—Poetry. | American poetry—21st century. | LCGFT: Autobiographical poetry.
Classification: LCC PS3612.I34475 P45 2021 | DDC 811/.6—dc23

Cover artwork: okanakdeniz/Shutterstock.com
Cover and interior text design by Ryan Scheife, Mayfly Design
First Edition 2021, Printed in the United States of America

CavanKerry Press is grateful for the support it receives from the New Jersey State Council on the Arts.

To Betsy Sholl, teacher and friend

Contents

Foreword

Welcoming a poet's first book into the world is a task both serious and joyous. The words within are pressurized by all that has been discarded, attempted, and discovered in the writer's lived and written experience. There are hours of doggedness and bright sparks of delight written into every page, every poem. What has been left out? So much. What remains in the winnowing? So much, again . . . and so richly compressed.

When a poet is "emerging" as an adult with a full, varied, and well-lived life behind her, as is Kali Lightfoot, the depth of delight is that much greater. Audre Lorde wrote, "Our visions are essential to create that which has never been, and we must each learn to use all of who we are to achieve those visions." Kali has been (and is) a wilderness ranger, stepmother, lesbian, educational leader, recovering alcoholic, grandmother, psychotherapist, and more. All of these identities come into the poems of *Pelted by Flowers*, which is roughly broken into sections that engage with aspects of self. Together, these voices create a unique and vital chorus, an affirmation of a life and an invitation to readers to consider their own whole and varied selves.

What's more, this vision is offered with deft art. Take, for example, the collection's debut poem, "Cousin Margaret's Friend, 1955," which offers a child's perspective on a tacitly lesbian relationship witnessed fifteen years before Stonewall:

Margaret's friend lightly touched her
shoulder, then filled the space
beside her, smiled, and shook
my father's hand . . .

It's the quiet drama of the line breaks here that convey the intensity of the moment. "Shook"—yes, the father's hand, but also the speaker's world and perhaps the parents' world, too. And this woman "filled the space" of so much more. The gift of the poet as a girl having seen a loving lesbian couple, accepted although unacknowledged by her family, is complicated and nuanced in Lightfoot's sensitive lines.

Eavan Boland said once, "the past is not the same as history. . . . History was so often a story of heroes. . . . but the past is a place of whispers and shadows." But whispers and shadows hold everything: memory and questions—as well as how those personal moments touch upon the Histories of our time. Poetry holds those shadows and makes of them light. We trust poems to bring mind and memory and heart into conversation and reckoning. I see that integration in Kali Lightfoot's poems.

What's more, we vitally need the voices of our foremothers to remind us what it was (and, in many places and lives, still is) to discover one's sexuality in the shadows or to buck the prejudices and bigotries of an era. Lightfoot's poems, even more importantly, don't stay in that past. They are a bridge to the present—a present in which the poet listens to Alicia Keys and reflects upon the economic engine of witch tourism in Salem, Massachusetts. These poems offer a bright testimony of survival and delight.

Lightfoot's trail-based and wild-space poems borrow from the spare work of Gary Snyder and the forms of traditional Japanese poetry, but again and again, it's the human that inspires her. Whether it's the trail boss, the weary hiker being led, the patient on a couch, or the old lover, this is a book of relationships. Between selves, people, the known and experienced, the past and present.

In the end, it's the wit of Lightfoot's work that freshens again and again. Take for example, the opening of "Wintry," its charmingly stilted delivery, its awareness and vulnerability:

I have had neither snow nor sex in a very long time, though snow came more recently than the opportunity to be naked in another's arms; and I say *another* instead of woman because at this point it is silly to discriminate.

And "(1944–   )," which takes the familiar "upon my death" poetic contemplation and imbues it with much-needed humor and perspective:

On a day filled with sun or clouds,
at the beginning of winter, or the end
of summer, in the middle of a poem
or slogging on foot through a snowstorm,
I will bump into my parenthesis.

No melodrama here, just alert amusement. This is the voice of one who has survived many of life's intensities and is curious and open about what they all might mean as they sing, together, through the chambers of the past and into the present.

Elizabeth Bradfield
North Truro
August 2020

Cousin Margaret's Friend, 1955

Cousin Margaret opened her door, smiling.
A sweater wrapped tight around her,
she spoke of the chill in Miami that day.
Pale, fey woman, shy with us—
her cousins from the North—an exotic bird
who might at any moment disappear.

Margaret's friend lightly touched her
shoulder, then filled the space
beside her, smiled, and shook
my father's hand. They led us to the parlor
for coffee and pie. We balanced china
plates and cups, the adults "catching up."
The friend promised to take me
to her pet store, making her my hero,
I, the kid who "rescued" sick birds
from our yard back home.

Later my dad and the friend went out back,
laughing together, ripping the husks
from coconuts on a sharpened metal stake,
tall and lethal. Next morning after breakfast
a young man knocked, whisked into the parlor
by Margaret's friend, murmuring head to head,
poring over charts. *Her bookie,* my mom
whispered. *She's betting on the horses!*
We all went to Hialeah Racetrack that afternoon.

This was years before Cousin Margaret died.
A bum ticker, my dad said.
Margaret's friend sat in her car outside
her pet store with an old rag stuffed

in the exhaust pipe. Mom and Dad
just clucked their tongues and exchanged a glance.

Half my life went by before I understood.
Now I too have loved a woman and lost
her to death. But not to silence—

I wish I could sit in the parlor
with Margaret's friend, ask how they met,
ask about their life together, push aside
the china cups and take her hand.
I wish I knew her name.

Picnic

Lake Michigan always terrified me—a wave could
knock me down, or swell pin me to the bluff

for I was a child "too sensitive" to enjoy a day at the beach
when the wind came up and clouds gathered at the edge

of sky, massing to race across the lake from Illinois
to chase me down before I could climb the long wooden

stairs from the beach to our car on the bluff above.
Thunder growled, quiet like my cat when I pulled his ears—

warning, warning—then grew and moved toward me,
winds flattening and building new waves, ever larger

as we packed up baskets, blankets, and towels.
My parents, laughing, took too much time,

caring nothing for the bully waves, the monster lion
rumbling closer in the clouds, ready to pounce.

I ran for the stairs, trembling, wide-eyed, only to fall
when the towel around my waist tangled my legs.

I cried. My dad scooped me up and carried me up the stairs,
thinking I must be hurt, surprised when we got into the car

to find that I was fine, no cuts or bruises. *There now,*
no reason to be crying, is there? I decided not to risk

new teasing, and shut my eyes when the hungry
lion spit frustration across our windshield.

Puberty, 1956

I was 12 and wanted to learn to play Schumann's "Träumerei"
on the piano. We didn't have a piano, and I couldn't even play
"Chopsticks," but like composer Robert, I wanted to sit on the bench

with Clara Schumann. Well, actually I wanted to be close
to Katharine Hepburn, who played Clara, and the piano,
in *Song of Love*. That year I also wanted to waltz barefoot

with Deborah Kerr in *The King and I,* comfort Ingrid Bergman
in *Anastasia*. And I imagined June Allyson's husky voice speaking
to me alone. I wept, dreamt, and had a crush on my counselor

at summer camp. Watching July Fourth fireworks with my best friend
Madeline, I offered to stand close to keep her warm, and laid
my trembling nonchalant arm across her shoulders.

A gut-twisting sense of wrongness warred with my pleasure
of touching her body. I stayed away from her for all the next day,
rode my bike to the library, and for the first time felt afraid of myself.

Because Earth is tilted 23½ degrees

seasons change with the angle of sunlight.
My sixth-grade teacher said we got this way
when Earth was young—a very big thing

called Theia slammed into her,w
tipped her, and sent rubble into orbit
that made our moon.

Adding color, Mr. Hoffman said
once in awhile Earth wobbles as it loops
around the sun, and bad things happen—

I pictured a Tilt-a-Whirl and our bodies
spinning off the sides. Grown up, I know
awhile is thousands of years, and weather

the only change—but the wobble joined
my collection of preadolescent worries:
giant spiders rising from the dark,

the progression from my period
to *heavy petting* to *going all the way*,
losing my virginity, not losing

my virginity, the atom bomb
in Russian hands, the hydrogen bomb,
the neutron bomb, and gamma rays

from exploding stars that might one day
in a direct hit wipe me out waiting
in line for the Ferris wheel.

At Seventeen

Remember me
from Junior Symphony?
I played trumpet flourishes,
you played the bassoon—
ungainly pipe of exotic beauty.

Old glowing wood and ivory,
metal keys, long curving metal tube
and double reed
that ended in your mouth,
Elena McCloud.

Your breath
gave us the sound
of ancient forests
moaning in the wind
and gnarled trees laughing
at the antics of magical beasts.

Even during rehearsal breaks
the reed was in your mouth,
nestled in a corner
staying moist.
You made your own,
a fiddly, persnickety process
of shaving bamboo
and wrapping it
in special twine.

Are you teaching
music somewhere, laughing
a deep, rich, bassoon laugh?
I loved you, Elena McCloud,

the person of you,
the sound
of you, though I didn't
know it then.
I could not have known it then,
had no words
to talk about it then.

It took years to learn
the language of myself,
to accept my love of women,
and understand the place
your music took me,
sitting amid the brass
and wind
and complicated strings.

Paterfamilias

after Kay Ryan's "He Lit a Fire with Icicles"

Angers, less predictable than thunderstorms,
roiled up in him like dry ice, smoky and harsh;
he pounded counters, slammed doors, stomped

hardwood floors. When the fury dispersed, it chilled
but never burned us, the family seated at his table.
My father was the cold of a Michigan snowstorm

blowing in from the Lake, making my shoulders hunch
against the wind, the cold of distance, the hug
that rarely came, quick kiss on my cheek on a winter

morning—offhand good-bye, his mind on work.
His friends say he was proud of me—for school studies
or the music I suppose, though he never said.

We laughed with him at stories that we knew by heart:
his days in the lumberyard before college, his Grandpa
Mitchell, the Scottish farmer full of verse.

There were no stories of his own father, George—
the drink, his disappearance—not even a phantom
at memory's family table.

My father built Mom's kitchen cabinets,
was city handball champion at age 50, served
in both World Wars, wrote poetry, coached football.

I doubt that I will ever feel as safe as I did then, sheltered
by him. But fear of him lives on, tucked in
beside that crazy wrath he taught me without knowing,

the cold in him that lit a fire in me, a rage I carry that matches his.
He sits on the other side of it, warming his hands,
watching me warm mine.

Genealogy

Gary, South Dakota, current population 225

H. B. Gary, my father's grandfather,
drove the first train into a small settlement
in 1873. Jubilant rail VIPs named it Gary
in honor of H. B., a man worthy of esteem.

George Gary, my grandfather, drunken fucker
if ever there was one, left when my dad was six.
Twenty years later he stumbled into a hospital
in Minnesota. He died in 1926 of liver cirrhosis.

But I bonded with George—his daughter's whispers
about him—when I was in rehab at Mercy Hospital.
I learned genes for addiction are inherited, and I was
hurtling to his fate if I didn't stop drinking. To drown

out the sorrows and rages of my rehab-mates, I told
myself sad little tales, fiddling with the few facts
I knew of George. A favorite was a fiction of him as
proxy for dead H. B. at the 50th anniversary of Gary:

the mayor stood proud in a black Sunday suit
on a wood platform. George in borrowed engineer
overalls tilted in a prairie wind, dust moving like
the ocean past his puzzled, rheumy eyes.

A new sign for the 50th read Gary, South Dakota
was "known far and wide as a place to have fun."
George did have fun—and a girl—in every town.
And a wife and three kids.

If I went to Gary, would I recognize an ancestral
eyebrow, or a nose, or one of these flat Gary thumbs

picking up a forkful of lemon pie at church supper?
Perhaps there'd be old copper pots in the kitchen

for beans or hearty beef stew. Beef on the hoof
runs through town now and then. I'd like to see
one of those cattle drives—dusty longhorns making
a stop at the lake for a long wind-soaked drink—

cattle, like George, thirsty after all those miles
run from home to nowhere they recognized.

Brain Tumor

Mom's head imploded. A stroke?
Tumor, they said, *surgery will save her*.

1966. No CAT scans nor MRIs, not much
but sharp knives, and phenobarbital

for the seizures. It made her sleepy.
She drank gallons of strong coffee

after they made the holes in her brain.
Her personality may change, they said,

and didn't say everything would change—
excellent cook losing track of ingredients,

sense of words in sentences, her own right foot.
Your mother healed better than anyone,

they said of the changeling who came home with us.
I loved her courage, her determination.

I started calling her *Mother* then,
the woman who wasn't ever again my *Mom*.

A Study in Consequence

I grew up under elm trees, four solid giants
who stood between sidewalk and street
with roots that heaved cement like February.

Step on a crack, you'll break your mother's back.

We tiptoed from house to house
over the root-cracks, chanted to each other
in *Bad Seed* voices, quavering our little
soupçon of possible evil,
                                        heads full
of Brothers Grimm and nasty stepmothers,
dark tales of captured children,
and unreliable wizards.
                              The elms all died
one summer from Dutch elm disease,
but still we avoided the sidewalk cracks
that never healed
                        and my mother's back
remained intact so who's to say
there wasn't magic there.

            I wish now we'd had
a prophylactic rhyme
for the real-life hazard that felled her.

Step out in the rain, you'll scramble
your mother's brain.

Petit Mal

My father's quatrains rhymed
AABB, iambs marching in imperfect
tetrameter, football epics he performed
at city breakfasts before the Big Game

and retirement roasts he shared
with fellow Kiwanians and university staff.
His poems never fished for what might
be swimming deeper. He wrote letters to me

away at grad school the year he died, jovial
raconteur voice speaking of chores done,
friends visited, and tending his garden:
forty-eight tomato plants, rows of beans

and broccoli, lettuce, potatoes, and corn.
He wrote to me hilarious stories
of his annual battles to protect the produce
from marauding rabbits and hornworm.

He made no mention of Mother's illness,
of how he felt about hearing her struggle
with words as he knelt to tie her shoes.
Or the petit mal seizures that dropped her

boneless to the sidewalk.
Did he think me too young to hear those things,
or were the words too hard to write?
My sister wishes he'd lived to swap tales

with his friends at the donut shop,
talking trash about any team sport's season.
I wish he had lived to talk to me
when I finally grew up enough to listen.

The Day Before

What is this day like for you?
The last day before you hear
test results: gene mutation

or not, disability
or not, early death
or not, or

not—the last
last day of 50% chances
before the days of 0% or 100%.

Did you have eggs Benedict
for breakfast? Are you thinking
about tacos for lunch?

Clutching this last day of mystery,
or anxious for certainty?
Betting on yes, or betting on no?

We aren't talking about genes
today or the doctor's appointment,
or the way your words

slur sometimes, your leg jerks.
Does Huntington's, or fear of it,
knot your muscles?

Last days are most often lived
backward—in memory of who
we were and what our lives

were like the day before Dad
died, or the fire took our house,
or I landed in detox.

This time we are living forward—
this isn't just Tuesday;
it's the Tuesday before we know.

The Day After We Heard the Results

Golden Shovel from "Of Seasonality" by Elizabeth Bradfield

It is facile to think *no, not this again*—
it isn't *this again*, it is *this* brand new—I
don't know who to be, or how I am
going to be anything but bumbling
wrong-footed, mis-weighted,
sad on this path, familiar and yet so strange.

Paula, Dying of Huntington's

In this, my seventy-second year,
I realize you were the love of my life.
I have been in love with others

since, but none whose inner child
played so well with mine.
None who loved my vocabulary

nor found me funny,
nor believed the shaman
who told us that my destiny

is to go through life as the Holy Fool.
Too bad your grownup self
was crazy as a bedbug,

and as nimble bed to bed,
landing finally with that guy
who offered you S and M

and a trip to Denmark to meet his family.
I still have the Danish paper stars
you folded for me that Christmas.

I would have stayed, you know,
all the way through to the end,
even knowing we were over,

the fireworks of intimacy dead,
all we had ahead to live the long
denouement of disease.

But you had the mad dark grace
to sleep with the Dane
and extricate us both.

The day I moved out, we said
good-bye, and hugged—sadly
civilized women making the best.

You closed the door.
I walked away
but had to return for my jacket,

forgotten in our farewells.
The door opened; my dry
wide eyes found you sobbing.

II

Jazz Hands

If forests

are the lungs

of the world   then leaves

are songs   trees breathe

soft breaths   pause

between words   inhaled stars

exhaled light   miracles

jazz hands   laughter

wet kisses

tears sent up

from the underworld

First Day in the Wilderness Area, Mount Adams, Washington

It's a long hike from the trailhead
to Looking Glass Lake, "lake" a misnomer
for this little tub of lava rock

catching rain so prettily in the foreground
of Mount Adams. 6000 feet of lonely glacier
hang there above the lake and me.

Never have I been here before this long day
in this green uniform with newly
minted badge and name tag. I shine with

bravado only possible to the truly clueless.
Never alone like this, backpacking
all by myself, the sun setting

behind all that hard-packed snow
in 38,000 acres of wilderness.
Little alpine flowers cling

to the rock by the lake. I cling
to my tent pole, thinking too much
about the little pile of bear scat, blue

from huckleberries, bear-eaten joyfully
no doubt—was he ambling through this lovely
scene sometime not too long before right now?

I am about to pitch this tent, a few hundredths
of a millimeter of ripstop nylon
between me and bears, wind, snow, rain, darkness,

and myriad things that walk
in the night. A dead branch drops,
pings against the lava rock, spits itself

into Looking Glass the almost-lake,
and startles me. Wide-eyed, I the almost-ranger
wonder if I'll see a second day.

Wilderness Ranger

[*haiku*]

ice axe
in the snow with
columbine

snow frosts
reds and golds
of autumn

steaming pile
of berry-stained scat—
bear ahead

krummholz lean
away from the wind
at timberline

[*senryu*]

krummholz
wood like living rock
at timberline

walking all of the
switchbacks shows maturity . . .
or sore knees

bannock
hard salami macaroni trail mix
cheese   repeat

one layer
of ripstop nylon between
me and the dark

[*tanka*]

ten days in wild air
my nose wrinkles
smelling oiled and dusty
logging road half a mile
ahead of me.

Gotchen Creek Guard Station, 3 a.m.

Sound, like a saw ripping through the wood floor,
pulls me out of sleep and out the door,
bucket of rocks in one hand, flashlight in the other.

Clothed in skin and outrage, I turn and crouch,
peer into the crawl space beneath the cabin—
three pairs of eyes flash behind spiderwebs—

I swat mosquitoes. The porcupines turn away,
chew on joists again, every chomp
rasps into the clearing. They seek

tree oils and salt in creosoted beams
but after three nights of cacophony,
their mission feels personal. No porcupine

spirit animal for me, no quilled totem
of innocent playfulness. Last night I poked them
with a broom—they moved deeper to new wood.

Today I collected creek stones, chose carefully
for weight and shape. I lob one. Eyes swing
back to me—six flat bright discs blink;

heads lower, quills rise, bodies hunker. They stare.
I swat. In unison they turn back to the joists.
Crazed primate, wilderness guard, protector of wildlife,

I pitch stone after stone. They chew, rise
and amble from the crawl space into meadow grass
lit by a clear half-moon. Behind me a twig snaps—
I remember I'm afraid of the dark—and naked.

Clement Powell Butte, Grand Canyon, September 3, 1872

pocket
   mouse
      skitters
down
daytime
burrow

butte
black
against coral
sunrise

The Powell Expedition, shouting to each other,
some of the first white men down the Colorado,
are busy making maps, journals, photographs:
from boats, on land, through dusty clefts
across the tumult of rock. Running rapids
with jubilant cheers, naming—
for themselves, their friends, sundry gods—
every prominence.

butte
gray
in purple
dusk

pocket
   mouse
      stirs
watches
hawk settle
into night

Mountain Dharma

Misery is a given—it's everything else you came for.

—Anne Dellenbaugh, owner of Her Wild Song:
Wilderness Journeys for Women

Steep ascent in the first half-mile, before beginners
feel good in their boots, inured to packs. Then the rain
starts. The trail a sudden creek, rocks cased in mud, clay

like sheet ice, weight of the pack a force in wrong directions.
It occurs to me that I carry my pack an hour longer than you
there at the head of the line. Not complaining, mind you,

I like walking sweep, nobody behind to step on my heels.
I stop and look at bits of the world you never see, rocketing along
at the front: a fine mushroom, tiny purple flower, two trees

grown together, or shiny shards of rock—arrowheads perhaps.
Coleaders we are, but at the back I plod slower than my legs
would like, cheering the walking wounded, becoming expert

on foot care, blister treatment. Our hike explores the *dharma*
of mountains, and ourselves: *intrinsic nature, essential quality,
character.* Forty miles to the top of Mount Katahdin,

you and I as much seekers as the women we shepherd.
We stragglers make camp in the dark, wet our intrinsic nature,
squirming nylon tent ropes, stakes loose in rain-soaked loam.

Blue morning sky struggles from behind thin clouds
as we, damp in our bones, crawl into the sun, walk sleepily
out of drippy woods to our kitchen on a granite ledge

beside a little teardrop pond, trees around us hung with last
leaves of autumn—a surprise we couldn't see last night,
perfect for our first morning meditation on dharma.

It takes a moment for our eyes to find the moose standing
shoulder deep in the pond, basking in sun, oblivious to us.
She ducks her head, snorts, waggles a bit, splashes water

flashing with rainbows as light shines through droplets flurrying
around her. We stand silent while she grazes idly on floating
pondweed, splashes again, unconcerned with the statues

we have become. Finally she turns to shore, wades through weeds
to scrubby woods, shakes herself, and strolls on knobby legs
into the shrubbery, heading off to perform her essential daily acts.

In Service to the Forest

I. Fire Camp—Oregon 1974

Free shirts, free cigars, free candy bars, free paper sleeping bags like the bags that keep ice cream cold but these keep us warm. 6 p.m. to 6 a.m. shift. Dinner at 5:30, get on the bus, go somewhere—all the somewheres look the same—blackened Douglas fir—some still standing—those are the dangerous ones that might be burned out inside from the roots but still look fine and healthy. When we get off the bus, someone hands us each a tool—shovel or Pulaski—and we walk single file along the lines of fire hose. In twos or threes, we stop at junctions and follow each line to its end, its metal wand. We hosey for the wand, the easiest job, and work in our small area, digging, chopping brush and branches, shoving the wand into the ground six inches. 12 hours. At midnight, lunch. We tell each other the C rations are from World War II. At 3 a.m. we find a little patch of fire in a fallen tree, turn our headlamps off, and sit to warm our hands. The bosses can't see us with our headlamps off. Later I fall asleep standing, leaning on my shovel. 5:30 a.m. We get back on the bus, back to camp for breakfast. Try to sleep in our paper bags, too hot, too much light, nothing to do—we trade candy for cigars, start rumors, pass rumors along—*There's a big fire in Alaska, they're going to take us to wash our clothes then send us up there*—try to get the commissary to give us more shirts. We laugh to hear that the air support bomber mistook grazing white sheep in a meadow for "smokes" and dropped fire retardant on them. We laugh to think of sheep dyed pink with their legs splayed out straight. The story gets less funny the more it's told, but we laugh louder each time.

II. Mop-Up

He saunters up beside me, belly brimming over the belt of his clean green pants—mine have mud up to the knees. He stares at me bent over my government issue shovel. *I guess it's okay to have you girls on the fire line, but how fast can you run?* I stare. This Line Boss wears a tin fire helmet like mine, but mine has M.A.R.S. (Mount Adams Ranger Station) stenciled on it. Four young women and four young men with shoulder-length hair might as well be from the planet Mars to the Fire Bosses and Line Bosses—our officers, the lifers—and we are this fiery planet's mop-up infantry spending our days watering and digging up ground the wildfire has burned across. We make mud pies of forest humus, douse leftover smokes before they can blow up into fires again. We dig and chop. I look at the Boss and think *How fast can YOU run?* But it's 1974 so I just stare.

III. Timber Crew—M.A.R.S. Washington State 1974

The District Ranger calls me into his office to give me my new assignment. *There's still too much snow to backpack in the Wilderness Area, I'm loaning you to the Timber Crew as tallyman—it's a hard job, the crew isn't sure a woman can do it, you will be the first.* Timber Crew: five guys with axes, their job to estimate the number of board feet, timber on the root, growing on this patch of land so the Forest Service can contract with a logging company to cut it. I ride out to the job with the crew bantering around me, not with me. The crew leader hands me the tallyman's clipboard, points to the paper clipped there, and tells me the guys will call out numbers to me and I will write them down. The men and I spread out through the forest. We walk in the same general direction, they use their axes to cut through vines and brush standing in their way. They call out numbers. I write them down. At lunch they throw their axes at a tree, compete for the best throw, closest to the middle. We walk some more, they call out numbers, I write them down. The leader calls a break, the man closest to me turns his back and runs to join his buddies. It is a hard job for a woman.

Kyoto

Sharing sake, singing
to the cherry trees, businessmen sit
in a park on tarps.

Children run
through fallen blossoms, laughing,
tossing them like fall leaves.

Sanjūsangen-dō Temple:
1001 gold-skinned statues of Kannon
shimmer in spring twilight.

On the Philosopher's Path, loose petals
dance among a thousand feet.

Shoulder Season

The weight of fall is in the clothes, a jacket
or light fleece, the thicker socks inside

my shoes, these longer pants, capris gone—
their summer glimpse of tanned, bare feet on sand.

I wait for scarlet maple trees to let
their color flutter down, polka-dot the street,

and stand denuded black against gray clouds.
November's rain turns into winter's snow,

its quiet flakes a mimicry of leaves
in their descent—afloat, not yet the barrier

nor slickness underfoot, more visual
than physical, they melt almost before

they land. I hunch my back, lean into winds,
feel the weight of early dark, oughts and shoulds,

had betters, musts and obligations, all
that slid unmet from naked summer shoulders.

Voice of Solitude

On a winter visit to Walden Pond, I learned
that a rock thrown onto the frozen surface
made a booming sound like a kettledrum.

I imagined Henry David Thoreau,
a man fond of solitude and of dramatic phrases,
shouting as he pitched an occasional rock
from his beach onto the icy pond:

To be awake is to be alive.

    BOOM

If a man does not keep pace with his companions,
perhaps it is because he hears a different drummer.

        BOOM

The mass of men lead lives of quiet desperation.

        BOOM

Years later, a wilderness ranger, I made room for
his weighty voice in my backpack among coffee
and camp stove, macaroni and gorp. Five days alone
among 38,000 acres of trees, lava rock, and snowfields,
in dawning awareness that Thoreau, spokesman
for solitude, walked into Concord every night—
a mile in well-traveled darkness—to dine
with family and friends, trade lofty thoughts
on life in the woods—and once a week
dropped his laundry off at his mom's.

Donkey Riding on Lesvos

This little beast, forty-five in human years,
carries me without complaint. Rhythm
of four feet, strange at first, beats
counterpoint for the two feet I'm used to.

Teetering on the scrap of saddle, I finally
square without thinking, rocking in time
to sounds of her hooves on hardpan trail.
No jets scream overhead—in fact

no motors at all compete
with the wind, or the shouts of Ares,
the drover: *Ela! Ela! Annabelle, ela!*
with burr of tongue and lips that seem

to say *I see you munching flowers
there! Get back to work.* I suspect
he chirrups at us as well: *Ela! Ela!
Sit straight, to the front, hold the reins!*

We could be walking anywhere
in time, among a thousand shades
of green that stretch across once-violent
hills to the Aegean. Ghosts of invading

Turks or Persians might even now
be standing under olive trees below us,
swords raised, waiting for our swaying
line to blunder into reach.

Annabelle, oblivious to my imagined
dangers, plods along unconcerned, dreaming
of tasty blooms. Her ears snap at Ares,
his chirps, and showy irritation.

Released by rhythm of hooves and voice,
my mind reaches lazy over a gate,
finds the latch and floats above
a garden, green hills, olive groves, the sea.

Wilmington, North Carolina

[*haiku*]

humid day
crepe myrtle
shimmers

clouds stack up
on the beach   rain falls
in waves

[*senryu*]

6 a.m.
dogs walk their humans
cats wash themselves

Spanish moss
like hanging coral reefs
in tidal air

crepe
myrtle   pink so loud
it startles me!

[*tanka*]

smooth sand
shells—scraggy boulders?
barnacles?
this beach seems
too easy

eating an ice cream
on this sunny autumn day
I long to hold
my grandson's
sticky hand

Ninety Degrees

All Things Considered mutters
to itself from the bedroom radio.
Air moves from the conditioner
out the guest room door
through a fan in the hall and arrives
halfhearted at the desk in the living room
where a writer sits thinking
of new ways to say *hot*,
humid. The room is dark
from narrow-slatted miniblinds
closed tightly against sun beating
on a whole scorching rank of windows.
NPR wafts in to announce the sale
of a painting Gauguin made
in South Pacific breezes
a hundred years ago.

The writer muses on Gauguin,
or more to the point, his women
on the beach in Tahiti dressed only,
if at all, in bright-colored cloth
wrapped below their waists,
breasts high and round,
long dark hair pulled back
from their faces. Unbidden,
the flab-chested homeless guy
who yesterday sat on a stoop
across from the bookstore
swims into view, shirtless,
stomach hanging over his belt,
chasing the Tahitians into the trees
behind the beach—

where the air surely is cooler.
The writer sighs, stands up,
flaps the hem of her T-shirt and walks to
the kitchen for a glass of cool, iced,
glacial, brisk, crisp, bracing water.

Haibun—Salt Marsh at Sandy Neck

Wet foot, dry foot, wet foot. Cordgrass, spike grass, salt meadow hay; summer greens shade to fall gold patched in red glasswort. We walk the marsh in each other's footsteps. Osprey nest a marvel of twigs, rope, bits of cloth. Salty grass, taste of salt on our tongues. Sulphurous scent of September's decay meets briny tangs on incoming tide. Killifish, horseshoe crabs little and big, moon snails, oysters, mermaid's toenail, squid eggs, blue heron, skate eggs, deer.

names of flowers
vanish just as fast as names
of friends

Cape Cod Meander

Round Pond—chubby crescent,
bitten moon. Slough Pond—
Slaow, not *Sluff* nor *Slew*.
Herring Pond—home to trout,
alewife, and bass; was ever
there a herring here? Wellfleet
glacier kettles filled with water
hidden from a thirsty sea.

Plop—green turtle drops
from rock, chitter of chipmunk,
chickadee-dee-dee
calls across years and memory
of Madeline and me, young seekers
in our Michigan woodland—
maple, beech, and basswood.
Young sassafras and sumac were
our size—we chewed bright-tasting
mitten-leaves, picked apart
red berries, tried to sit quiet
with her father, looking
for ring-necked pheasants.

Wellfleet birds watch me
then rise and flutter off—
I hear but rarely see them,
like pheasants all those
years ago. I brush through sumac,
tear off a mitten leaf to chew,
wonder where Madeline might be
now—and almost miss
a fox darting among autumn
leaves: orange blur of body,
swish of tail, gone.

Late Autumn

Scarlet leaves on a shrub beside the brick garage
dazzle walkers hunched in fleece and scarves.

Fore River water mimes an ice blue sky. Next month
steam will rise—winter's gift to morning.

IV

Career Change

During their hour spent on the flowered
couch, my leather chair facing them,
box of tissues prominent
on the table between us,
I sat with shattered souls who sought
me for mending what was torn in them.

Stories horrible to listen to
conjured pictures I didn't want
etched into my memory.
I learned the latest
therapeutic strategies,
but in the end I knew the only tool
that truly healed was listening.

I held open in that pleasant room
exquisite silence where a ragged
soul might knit itself together,
and ever so slowly I unraveled.

Mystery

The second step we take in AA
is to believe in a power
greater than ourselves.
Newly sober, I tried to trust

in a peaceful alpine meadow,
then the love of the AA group itself;
later I embraced the Eastern pantheon,
so different from the trinity

I had tried and failed to love.
I learned Sanskrit chants and poems.
But one day in meditation noticed
that no matter how many verses

I sang to the guru's sandals,
it was always You who showed up,
looking like Charlton Heston
in *The Ten Commandments*

and maybe a little like my dad:
tall, feet planted, eyes on the horizon,
the true man taking charge.
Though I am grateful to know

You at all, I would really like You
to show up as someone else:
Xena the Warrior Princess perhaps,
or Helen Mirren looking lovely—

a smart, strong woman in her 60s.
But I seem to be stuck with You,
the right-wing guy with granite
tablets in one arm and a rifle

in the other. You are not a God
of compassion or comfort,
but You are the God that has kept
me sober all these years.

At Roslindale Station

after "You Who Never Arrived" by Rainer Maria Rilke

You who never arrived in my arms,
beloved, simply missed the train, again.
I believe instead that it was something
I said, or did, or did not do, or should have
thought about if I had been smarter.

But you say your old rusted piece
of shit car just finally died and you
were running late as usual—I am
only one of the most recent thousand
things that capture your attention—

but not for long. So, at this moment
and from this moment to the next
that lives within it, I pledge to forgive
myself from responsibility—
not you, not yet, but myself.

There will be no further thought,
self-recrimination, or rehearsal
of guilt as I relive the misery
of that train chuffing into the station,
beloved, and you not arriving in my arms.

Family Court

I.

Everyone but Lucas cried
    the day he left the orphanage—

too small to know
    he wouldn't see that door again,

not old enough to know
    the Russian for *loss* or *future*,

he didn't know us,
    his new forever family.

II.

Two years and an ocean
    of paperwork later,

we gather—nuclear
    and extended clan:

thirteen of us file silent, smiling,
    into a room in need of smiles,

its everyday caseload a litany
    of divorce and disaffection.

The judge sits with us
    in the gallery, not behind her desk.

Lucas, do you like living with Mama and Papa?
    Yes.

Do you like having a new big brother?
    It's okay sometimes.

And Alexander, do you like having Lucas around?
    He rolls his eyes, mumbles something.

Mute, we hold our breaths, hope the judge remembers
    being young, has a sister.

She winks and speaks her official words,
    then lets Lucas bang her gavel
    to adopt us.

Three Seals

after Richie Hofmann

I. December 28, 2012, 1:25 a.m., City Hall, Portland, Maine

Two men stand on the top step, hold hands,
parkas unzipped to show matching T-shirts—
Love Is Love. Standing below them we cheer,
wave candles—they hold up their marriage license,
with its gold seal of the State of Maine,
first state where citizens' votes made gay marriage
legal. The first couple steps down
into hugs, pelted by flowers—we watch
for the next, prepared to cheer every pair,
our voices husky with cold.

II. A Summer Morning, Boothbay Harbor

Today in the quiet of purple dawn,
a harbor seal treads water
ten feet from my solo canoe,
onyx eyes fixed on me. I stare back,
watch nostril slits open, close,
open. We breathe together awhile.

III. November 12, 2016, Salem, Massachusetts

Our post office, built 1933, Colonial Revival
architecture so convincing I imagine
mailmen in three-corner hats and breeches
descend the graceful front stairs I climb
to mail another donation I can't afford—
this one for wilderness protection
follows others for civil liberties, racial justice,
reproductive rights. What to do on this day of feeling

unheard, unseen; what to do but lick the envelope,
seal my check inside, stop at the bronze slot
and tip the flap, feel a puff of air as my hopes
land with all the others there in the dark.

Reading a Lesbian Romance Novel on the Train to Salem

Settling into my seat and a parallel world,
I meet a beautiful A-list movie star who is
falling in love with my twenty-something
self—the lean, blond nanny she has just hired.

Three gawky young girls stumble
and giggle, making sure we all see them
on their way to the café car.

The A-lister is part Filipino
with dark alluring eyes and long lashes.
Her caramel skin looks lovely
against my creamy Irish hue.

I careen forward to the café car, zagging
in the aisle as the train zigs around a corner.
One of the girls spills Coke on my jeans.

A-lister has a five-year-old daughter—
smart, loving, articulate—
and a mysterious past. Of course
she is fabulously wealthy.

Oblivious fellow in front of me abruptly
leans his seat back, almost crushing
my coffee cup—and my knees.

I am in a private jet with A-lister and daughter
heading to their second home in Kauai,
this nanny summer a prelude to
starting my PhD in astrophysics.

The conductor leans over to say
something to another trainman.
They share a cynical laugh.

Now we are having wild hot sex in her fabulous
bathroom at her Hollywood Hills estate.
We were outed in Kauai by *People*
magazine and barely escaped the paparazzi.

In Salem today I will look at three condos and hope
I can afford one I like. Meanwhile, three possible
buyers will sniff around my Portland home.

Sipping wine on the veranda, we hold hands
and speak of our future as a family. I will finish
my PhD research, and we will make a second child
with sperm she purchases at a private Swiss clinic.

In Portland later today, I'll pay $3200 for car repairs.
Rain tomorrow—will the ceiling leak? I'll work
on retirement forms, play solitaire, and mop the floor.

On the Bench above Spring Point Light, Portland, Maine

Peaks Island Ferry chugs across the harbor.
Sailboats moored in middle distance swing
into the wind like weathervanes.

I lean back on a bronze plaque glinting
in afternoon sun: "Look for the Heaven
here on Earth. It is all around you."

This grassy hill is manmade, once a wartime
gun emplacement, concrete and steel
under wildflowers, now the guns long gone.

Fort Gorges faces me, gun ports empty,
on its rocky outcrop halfway to Peaks Island.
Civil War long over, the fort is covered in green.

Weapons placed here for strategic defense
never fired a shot at enemies who never arrived.
Anna and I sat here one summer night, the forts

disguised with loveliness: sweet pea and salvia
moving in warm wind, passersby smiling at us
in this place built for war and mayhem, forts

still waiting to take up arguments of guns.
We tried for beauty or peace, and found instead
the argument that ended us.

My Affair with Alicia Keys

I knew your name, but not the physics of you,
the physiognomy, the physicality until that night
I clicked on *The Voice* on Hulu and there you were,
shining eyes, the rows of braids, the scarf tied just so,
the flashy tunic that two of you could fit into,
fashion print, your platform shoes to make you
goddess-tall. I think there might have been two of you—
was that the season you were pregnant? You laughed
full-throat with your celeb judges, danced in your judging
chair. But what I loved, really loved, was you
with the fledglings, the singers trying so hard
to make a name, to be a celeb, to join their voices with yours.
I loved your focus on the song, leading the singer as though
you knew exactly what steps to take, what notes to bring forward,
how the drummer's rhythm matched her, how the band
could make her shine. That little singer you loved—
yes, it was obvious, even a little embarrassing,
how much you cared. Or maybe I was jealous,
yes, I fell in love too, with you, sitting with me in my living room
every week, bantering, teaching me to listen—does everyone
who watches feel this way, for an hour every week feel like
your friend, wish to be your student—is that what television
is really about? Am I meant to fall in love, to feel like
I have made a friend, that I am the equal of some mega-talented
musician paid oceans of dollars to sit and be famous,
and mentor someone else, never me? And did I mention the shoes,
the ones that glitter and make you taller than that very tall country singer,
the shoes more like a perch than a shoe, designer Jimmy or Christian?
I buy your CDs, read stories about you in glossy magazines,
and we never speak. I might write a note. I see you just bought
an Arizona mansion and a classic Thunderbird.

Wintry

after "Snow" by Mary Ruefle

I have had neither snow nor sex in a very long time, though snow came more recently than the opportunity to be naked in another's arms; and I say *another* instead of *woman* because at this point it is silly to discriminate. Just as every snowflake is a different pattern and most are lovely, it seems that would also be true of a human wanting to have sex with me and me wanting to have sex with her or him but more with her. And birds, what about birds? Not to have sex with, but it has also been a very long time since I have seen any bird except a seagull scudding past my window or, when I'm in the car, occasionally a hawk making attentive circles above 95, hunting but for less-than-obvious prey. Seeing a hawk makes me think of my vulnerable fleshy nakedness, even though at that moment of hurtling down the highway, I am surrounded by several thousand pounds of vehicle harder than a hawk's bill and an appropriate amount of cotton. More than birds though, I would like there to be snow outside this third-floor window flying on a northeast wind, and warm skin waiting in the next room to make love with me as soon as I finish typing these hard little letters.

V

Icarus Takes a Window Seat

Your voice on the phone
carries a rattle
of beverage carts,
seatbelts snapping,
and the frenzied beating
of your heart as you wait
for the door to close
and trap you.

I would like to say
the words to help you
but you've been
talking to Icarus
and Bellerophon.
You three boys
know with certainty
the hubris of flight.
Who am I
to contradict you?

Bellerophon fallen
from winged Pegasus
and Icarus blistered
in ecstatic wings.
From then to now
millennia of cautionary
tales speak doom
to those who fly,
and you in this instant
can hear them all.

You say you are a loser.
I say you are a hero.

Neither of us is right.
You are a panicked man
calling his bewildered mother.
Both anxious, both alive,
remembering two
dead Greeks
who wanted to see
the other side of the clouds.

Dear *New York Times*

The writer and poet Eileen Myles, who has spent the last four decades in relative obscurity, is now a muse for the popular Amazon series Transparent.

—*New York Times*, January 16, 2016

Relative *obscurity?* Eileen Myles? Icon of the gender queer/
the badass underrepresented/ author and midwife
of 20 books of prose and poetry—*Chelsea Girls* a classic—
presidential candidate/ hot punk dyke/ unafraid to speak truth
to power/ and her own truth/ no matter how unpopular/
even to her own underrepresented community/ and wear plaid
flannel before it became a thing/ and look like an unmade bed
before that became a thing. Maven of controversy/ happy to write
about sex/ to write about cats/ to write about whatever the hell.

Obscurity like 1993 when 8 of us drove to Washington, D.C. to join *hundreds of thousands* (said the *Washington Post*) for the Equal Rights March announced in liberal newspapers, *Gay Community News, Bay Windows*, Glad Day and New Words bookstores, Chaps and Somewhere and The Saints bars, and every other queer venue, and word of mouth across our neighborhoods? We stayed with Thom's sister in her big house near Rock Creek Park, played with her kids, commiserated about her messy divorce though none of us could get married let alone divorced. She looked at us in puzzlement at breakfast and asked,

But how did you all know about the march?

If any man or woeman be a witch,
(that is hath or consulteth with a familiar spirit,)
They shall be put to death.

> *I am afraid that ages will not wear off that reproach and those*
> *stains which these things will leave behind them upon our land.*

—Thomas Brattle, Salem, Massachusetts, October, 1692

Middle-schoolers shriek along cobblestones,
wear tags, each with the same word: Vampires.
A woman in seventeenth-century Puritan mufti

and Nike sneakers leaves CVS, collides with a devil
on his way into Coven's Cottage. The seven-foot zombie
who makes tourists scream and snap quick selfies

nods hello to Frankenstein seated by Witch City Tees,
wanders off to share a smoke with two guitar-playing pirates.
A troupe of actors in colonial costumes captures one of their own,

leads her to Old Town Hall for trial. Tourists in witch
hats and Red Sox caps follow, smiling.
Psychics, tarot card readers, aura photographers,

witches, and warlocks in robes and chains—the gold kind
with pentagrams—Pagans and prophets at tables in the mall.
The cloud of Vampires floats past a cloud of Werewolves.

Twenty tourists exit the Witch Museum. Five
laughing women sport sequined, beribboned witch hats.
Visiting evangelists yell about a vengeful God.

A month of Haunted Salem Happenings, then Halloween:
250,000 visitors—in 1692, 19 people were hanged by their
neighbors. Positive impact in 2015: $100 million.

Queer Nobility

FAIRY, the knotted face shouts
at me this morning from a dented car
racketing along Canal Street.

Stunned, confused, I think
Shouldn't that be faggot?
and then *Do I look like a gay man*

in my jeans, boots, corduroy shirt?
The construction worker from
the Village People, maybe?

But c'mon man, *fairy*
feels to me like *princess*
and I'm happy to make it my own:

Lezzie Princess . . . The Duchess
of Dyke . . . Butch Baroness . . .
Muff Diver to Her Majesty.

(1944–   )

On a day filled with sun or clouds,
at the beginning of winter, or the end
of summer, in the middle of a poem,
or slogging on foot through a snowstorm,
I will bump into my parenthesis.

Mary at 90 tripped over hers
last week on the steps of the art museum
where it tangled her rushing feet,
late for her docent job.

Mom's lay next to her
on the nursing home bed, waiting
patiently through coma for the last
long breath.

Dad's also met him lying down—
in peaceful sleep after a day
spent with sledge and splitting wedge
in the backyard.

Kevin, driving too fast in the Oregon
desert on graduation night,
saw his in the guise of the windshield
just before his head etched a star.

On this particular day at winter's end
I walk, coat open, sun warm
on my body, and a new spring arriving
after months of winter white and gray.

I Tune In News of the World

After all, what is reality anyway? Nothin' but a collective hunch.

—Jane Wagner/Lily Tomlin

Nine Pakistani police trainees died
this morning in a safe house
that was their dormitory.
Anonymous assassins
thought to be Taliban
killed them as they rose from bed.

Suspended in a thin silver bowl,
the entire known universe floats
on a glass-topped
coffee table covered with books
on architecture
in a room that overlooks a sea—
laughter drifts in from the deck.

Yesterday an avalanche in France:
ten mountain climbers buried
when warm winds on Mont Maudit,
"the cursed,"
loosed a plate of snow.

Humanity inhabits a flat disc
carried by four elephants who stand
on the back of a turtle slowly swimming
through the cosmos.
Death, a talking skeleton in a black robe,
rides a pale horse named Binky.

Treadmill . . . with Poetry

My feet begin their journey.
I settle headphones,
Jorie Graham between my ears.

Six TV screens overhead
different scenes, white
closed captions,

one with the CNN crawl—
Breaking News!
Law & Order on another,

sleazy defendant (shiny suit) winks
at horrified prosecution witness,
defense attorney stands stony,

closed caption doesn't comment.
Jorie reads her new poem, "The Mask Now,"
Dying, Dad wanted sunscreen. Nonstop. . . .

Schumer: GOP has no idea
how to replace Obamacare
crawls past. Erudite author

comments on poem, fight
breaks out on basketball court,
referee takes punch . . . nosebleed.

Ellen DeGeneres laughs
with Kerry Washington,
slim blond prosecutor purses

scarlet lips, caption states,
All charges are dropped. You are free to go.
Mr. Sleaze, even slimier, smiles, judge

looks hunted. *Breaking News:*
Chicago Police Speak on Torture Video.
The next poet clears his throat.

My therapist suggested walking
on treadmills at the YMCA when it's icy:
It's safer and you can still listen to poetry.

Requiem

A few words heading toward a line
born at the stoplight on Derby Street;

it was a quiet little idea. My eyes
fuzzed over and I could read it there

in that thinking place where lines
scroll by at odd moments.

No pen from the passenger seat,
no scramble for a scrap of paper—

I thought, *I will remember this,*
and I did recall it for awhile.

The light turned green.
I played with the line

and its follower
as I turned onto Lafayette,

spied a meter in front
of Winer Brothers Hardware,

parked and locked the car.
But my shopping list

stepped up and asserted
itself, scattering the still

tentative little collection
of words—now lost for good

behind a plug for the sink, two
screws, and an ironing board cover.

Melting Polar Ice Caps

In quiet dawn, grains of sand roll under small waves.
On windy mornings sand lifts and slides across the dunes.
Each grain was birthed from a stone washed

by the sea and pummeled by rivers scoured by wind.
We squish sand between our toes,
dive into booming surf, shriek and hoot

at the power of water breaking over us, walk
gratefully next to the sea in purple dawns.

We know the jargon of catastrophe: storm surge, destructive erosion,
flooding wetlands, lost habitat for animals and plants. The sea is rising.
Homes lost, property disappearing, plant life and animals driven inland,

but first to be eaten by the rising sea will be
mere sand—the beaches: playgrounds for a summer day,
places to sit in difficult hours and listen to the *ssshhh* of sand and water.

Children of a baby born today will watch every beach
be drowned by relentless ocean, water lap
against rock and pavement, flow
among roots of trees, waves break
against shingled walls of shorefront homes.

> No tourists will nap on a warm sand-held
> towel, take long moonlit walks.

Puppies will not chase sandpipers
now extinct.
> No habitat will house
> sand crabs, beachhoppers, olive snails,
> bean and razor and pismo clams, Pacific sand dollars,

sand stars, elbow crabs, or sea pansies—extinct,
no time for adaptation.

There will be no jobs for clam diggers, worm harvesters,
or hot dog vendors
who once served up a bit of sand with every bun.

Star Stuff

The apples will not care
that I didn't walk this morning
or never learned a second language
or read Proust
or was not a better supervisor.

Knowing that atoms of my body come from stars
that died five billion years ago
and will be available
five billion years from now in some other body
or star
or drop of water
or apple lying in the orchard path
is oddly comforting.

Red and purple sunsets from the bluff above the pond
or Katahdin on a full moon night
or "Silent Night" sung by candlelight
or the smiles of my grandsons
will be of no consequence to a drop of water.

I will be as dust drifting
on a solar wind,
beyond atmosphere
and planet, untroubled and unconscious.
This much-worried, much-loved life—
atoms strewn across a galaxy of galaxies.

Notes

First Day in the Wilderness Area, Mount Adams, Washington

In 1973 I was hired as the first woman wilderness guard or ranger, the titles were interchangeable, on Mount Adams. The federal Wilderness Act of 1964 created the wilderness areas by drawing a line around a wild area on a map and protecting it from human activity. It also created the job of wilderness ranger, a person to patrol the wilderness, in my case backpacking alone for five or ten days at a time. I did this for only two seasons, and a third in New Hampshire's White Mountains, but it has remained a central experience in my life.

In Service to the Forest

Because the main trails in the Mount Adams wilderness are at about 5000 feet on a glaciated dormant 12,000-foot volcano, the summer hiking season is short and can start as late as August and end in early September. The wilderness ranger becomes a sort of floater or utility outfielder, helping out on the fire crew, recreation crew, timber crew, or district office doing everything from fighting forest fires to filing paperwork, cleaning campgrounds, and measuring trees for logging contracts. In the early '70s I was often a female anomaly on those crews.

The Day Before

Huntington's disease is a fatal genetic disorder that causes the progressive breakdown of nerve cells in the brain. It deteriorates a person's physical and mental abilities during their prime working years and has no cure. It is the quintessential family disease because every child of a parent with the disease has a 50/50 chance of carrying the faulty gene (according to the Huntington's Disease Society of America). Diagnosis is made with genetic testing, which confirmed that my stepson had inherited the disease from his mother, my ex-partner.

If any man or woeman be a witch,
(that is hath or consulteth with a familiar spirit,)
They shall be put to death.

The original Body of Liberties of the Massachusetts Colony, the first legal code established by European colonists in New England in 1641, made witchcraft a capital offence. The first article of the capital code stated the provision for the punishment of idolatry, and I used the second article for the title of my poem.

https://history.hanover.edu/texts/masslib.html

I Tune In News of the World

The last stanza refers to characters in the *Discworld* series of books by Terry Pratchett.

Dear *New York Times*

The caption referred to in the epigraph can be found here:

https://www.nytimes.com/2016/01/17/fashion/eileen-myles-jill-soloway-girl friend-transparent.html

Acknowledgments

Thanks to the editors of the following publications in which the poems in this book first appeared, sometimes in slightly different versions:

Journals

Amethyst Review: "Mountain Dharma," "Mystery"
Failed Haiku: "Wilderness Ranger"
Gyroscope Review: "Three Seals," "Wintry"
Illuminations 29: "Donkey Riding on Lesvos"
Lavender Review: "At Roslindale Station," "First Day in the Wilderness Area, Mount Adams, Washington"
Lily Poetry Review: "I Tune In News of the World"
Molecule: "Jazz Hands"
Mom Egg Review: "Icarus Takes a Window Seat"
Montana Mouthful Literary Magazine: "Voice of Solitude"
Poetry South: "Cousin Margaret's Friend, 1955," "Wilderness Ranger"
Silver Birch Press: "At Seventeen" (as "First Love" in the "ME, At 17" series)
Snapdragon Journal: "The Day After We Heard the Results"
Split Rock Review: "Picnic"
Star 82 Review: "Haibun—Salt Marsh at Sandy Neck," "Queer Nobility"

Anthologies

Come Shining: Essays and Poems on Writing in a Dark Time: "Star Stuff" (Kelson Press)
Feminine Rising: "Puberty 1956" (Cynren Press)

The Wildest Peal: Contemporary Animal Poetry II: "Donkey Riding on Lesvos"
   (Moon Pie Press)

Thanks to the editors of *Lavender Review* for nominating "At Roslindale Station" for a Pushcart Prize.

Thanks to the editors of *Poetry South* for nominating "Cousin Margaret's Friend" for a Pushcart Prize.

I am also grateful to the judges of the SFPA Speculative Poetry Contest for awarding an honorable mention to "I Tune In the News of the World."

I am grateful to Sarah Franklin, who put line breaks in my email message and urged me to take Betsy Sholl's poetry workshop at the University of Southern Maine where I was an administrator. To Betsy, who let me take that class for four semesters and a summer session in Greece, and then encouraged me to apply for an MFA. To Fran Myers and Anne Cardale, who made it possible for me to take a phased retirement from USM. To Vermont College of Fine Arts, Louise Crowley, staff, faculty, and students for an MFA and experiences that changed my life—really! To my advisors at VCFA: Jen Bervin, Jody Gladding, Leslie Ullman, and David Wojahn. To Mary Snell for Greece; to Patricia Budd, Mary Snell, Janet Stebbins, and Dana Robbins for our biweekly workshop group in Portland. To all of the VCFA student-friends who remain in my life—and particularly my Facebook posse. To everyone who has dropped into and out of the monthly Poetry Cleanse. To the Maine Writers & Publishers Alliance and Mass Poetry for their support. To January Gill O'Neill, Cindy Veach, Jennifer Martelli, Kathleen Aguero, Jennifer Jean, Dawn Paul, Lis Horowitz, Colleen Michaels, Danielle Jones, Kevin Carey, and MP Carver for Thursdays at Gulu Gulu, and everything else. To my biweekly workshop group on the North Shore: Claire Keyes, Carol Seitchik, Priscilla Herrington, Robin Linn, and Susanna Brougham. To JD Scrimgeour for the Tuesday morning writers' studio at the Salem Athenaeum. To the Minnesota Northwoods Writers Conference, William Joiner Institute for the Study of War and Social Consequences Summer Writers' Workshop, the Fine Arts Work Center, and Wellfleet Bay Wildlife Sanctuary Field Schools for incredible learning opportunities. To Elizabeth Bradfield for writing the foreword to this collection, for founding Broadsided Press, and for her ongoing support and friendship. To Pamela Alexander, MP Carver, and Susanna Brougham for their time and comments on the manuscript of this collection. To Claudia Filos for my author photo and help with my website. To the people at CavanKerry Press for choosing to publish this book, and to Baron Wormser for shaping it, and Joy Arbor for her brilliant copyediting. Thank you to my father for his love of Ogden Nash and Robert Service; and my sister, Shirley, for always thinking I was a poet, even during the forty years when I didn't think I was one. To Laura and Paul Knight for their love and their enthusiasm for my journeys, wherever they might take me.

CavanKerry's Mission

A not-for-profit literary press serving art and community, CavanKerry is committed to expanding the reach of poetry and other fine literature to a general readership by publishing works that explore the emotional and psychological landscapes of everyday life, and to bringing that art to the underserved where they live, work, and receive services.

Other Books in the Emerging Voices Series

Red Canoe: Love In Its Making, Joan Cusack Handler
WE AREN'T WHO WE ARE and this world isn't either, Christine Korfhage
Imago, Joseph O. Legaspi
Through a Gate of Trees, Susan Jackson
Against Which, Ross Gay
The Silence of Men, Richard Jeffrey Newman
The Disheveled Bed, Andrea Carter Brown
The Fork Without Hunger, Laurie Lamon
The Singers I Prefer, Christian Barter
Momentum, Catherine Doty
An Imperfect Lover, Georgianna Orsini
Soft Box, Celia Bland
Rattle, Eloise Bruce
Eye Level: Fifty Histories, Christopher Matthews
GlOrious, Joan Cusack Handler
The Palace of Ashes, Sherry Fairchok
Silk Elegy, Sondra Gash
So Close, Peggy Penn
Kazimierz Square, Karen Chase
A Day This Lit, Howard Levy

Pelted by Flowers has been set in FreightSans Pro, the sans serif counterpart to the typeface FreightText. The humanist forms of FreightSans Pro give it a warm and friendly appearance. It was designed by Joshua Darden and published by GarageFonts in 2009.

This book was printed on paper from responsible sources.